SPOTLIGHT ON
IMMIGRATION AND MIGRATION

IMMIGRATION TO COLONIAL AMERICA

Jackie Heckt

PowerKiDS
press™

NEW YORK

Published in 2016 by The Rosen Publishing Group, Inc.
29 East 21st Street, New York, NY 10010

Editor: Caitie McAneney
Book Design: Samantha DeMartin / Andrea Davison-Bartolotta

Photo Credits: Cover SuperStock/Getty Images; p. 4 Library of Congress/Wikimedia Commons; pp. 5, 7 North
Wind Picture Archive; p. 6 Johannes Vingboons/Wikimedia Commons; pp. 8–9 White House/Wikimedia
Commons; pp. 10, 16–17 (main), 21 courtesy of Library of Congress; p. 11 Universal History Archive/Getty
Images; p. 12 Everett Historical/Shutterstock.com; p. 13 (inset) Kean Collection/Getty Images; p. 13 (main)
traveler1116/Getty Images; p. 14 William Jackson/BBC Paintings/Wikimedia Commons; pp. 15, 22 Ann Ronan
Pictures/Print Collector/Getty Images; p. 17 (inset) Boston Public Latin School/Wikimedia Commons; p. 18 U. S.
Capitol/Wikimedia Commons; p. 19 Fotosearch/Stringer/Getty Images; p. 20 Stock Montage/Getty Images.

Library of Congress Cataloging-in-Publication Data

Heckt, Jackie.
 Immigration to colonial America / Jackie Heckt.
    pages cm. — (Spotlight on immigration and migration)
 Includes index.
 ISBN 978-1-5081-4081-8 (pbk.)
 ISBN 978-1-5081-4082-5 (6 pack)
 ISBN 978-1-5081-4084-9 (library binding)
1. United States—History—Colonial period, ca. 1600-1775—Juvenile literature. 2. United States—Emigration
and immigration—History—Juvenile literature. 3. Immigrants—United States—History—Juvenile literature. I.
Title.
 E188.H39 2016
 305.9'06912097309032—dc23
                              2015023451

Manufactured in the United States of America

CPSIA Compliance Information: Batch #BW16PK: For further information contact Rosen Publishing, New York, New York at 1-800-237-9932.

CONTENTS

A New World 4

Establishing Colonies. 6

Freedom of Religion. 8

Encountering Native Tribes. 10

Farming in the South 12

Slavery Comes to America. 14

Life in Colonial New England 16

The Start of American Democracy 18

Immigrants to the Middle Colonies 20

Shaping a Nation. 22

Glossary 23

Index. 24

Primary Source List. 24

Websites. 24

A NEW WORLD

America is a land of **immigrants**. In fact, every American is either an immigrant or **descendent** of immigrants. The United States grew quickly thanks to the continual arrival of immigrants from around the world.

Christopher Columbus reached the Americas in the 1490s, and other explorers soon followed. In 1524, Italian explorer Giovanni da Verrazano became the first European to explore the East Coast of North America. Less than a century later, immigrants began to arrive from all over Europe. They came from places such as Spain, France, the Netherlands, and England. They came in search of a better life, free from religious and political **persecution**. They hoped to find wealth in the land's **resources**. These immigrants began to establish colonies in what they called the New World.

CHRISTOPHER COLUMBUS

In May 1539, Spanish explorer Hernando de Soto and his expedition landed on the coast of Florida. For years, the expedition explored inland North America and became the first known Europeans to cross the Mississippi River.

ESTABLISHING COLONIES

The first **permanent** European colony in North America was St. Augustine, in what is today's Florida. The Spanish established this colony in 1565. However, it was the British who later founded many of the colonies.

In 1587, one of Britain's first colonization attempts took place on Roanoke Island, off the coast of today's North Carolina. However, those colonists disappeared. In 1607, the British succeeded in setting up a colony at Jamestown, Virginia. The Pilgrims then founded Plymouth, Massachusetts, after arriving on the *Mayflower* in 1620. In 1626, Dutch settlers bought land from Native Americans and called it New Amsterdam. The British later took over this colony, naming it New York. By the 1730s, the British controlled the East Coast and had established 13 colonies there. Each colony **developed** its own identity.

NEW AMSTERDAM

The first immigrants to North America faced a rough, long journey on choppy waters. They didn't know what they'd find in this new land.

FREEDOM OF RELIGION

From its beginning, America was seen as a place of religious **tolerance**. In fact, one of the main reasons the Europeans flocked to America was religion. A period of religious unrest followed Great Britain's defeat of the Spanish navy in 1588. The British rulers forced their subjects to follow the Church of England.

The Pilgrims, who arrived in New England in 1620, included immigrants who came to America for economic reasons and others who were escaping religious persecution in Britain. They were fleeing King James I, who wouldn't recognize their religion. The Puritans also came to Massachusetts to escape persecution in Britain. Pennsylvania, which was colonized in 1681, became a safe place for the Quakers, a religious group known for their peaceful way of living.

Among the Pilgrims were Separatists, or people who wanted to split from the Church of England. Puritans wanted to change the Church of England to make it more pure. Both groups found religious freedom in America, but weren't always tolerant of people with different religious ideas.

ENCOUNTERING NATIVE TRIBES

European immigrants didn't know what they'd find in North America. Some dreamed of wealth and opportunity. They hoped to find gold as the Spanish had in South America. Instead, they found vast amounts of land populated by Native Americans.

The Indian nations **reacted** in different ways to the European settlers. Some were helpful, teaching the immigrants how to farm the land. Others weren't so friendly. The Native Americans around Jamestown came to view the immigrants with suspicion. The settlers stole food from Native Americans and occupied more and more land. Native Americans finally attacked the colonists. In the end, however, the newcomers forced the Native Americans to leave their home. They used guns and horses to drive Native Americans away and killed many more with **disease**.

MAP OF VIRGINIA, 1590

Their greene corn

John White was one of the first Englishmen to land on Roanoke Island and explore the Carolinas. He made watercolor paintings that gave the English an idea of how Native American tribes lived.

Their sitting at meate

The place of solemne prayer

horse wherin the Tombe of their Herounds standeth

11

FARMING IN THE SOUTH

Early European immigrants to Virginia wanted to strike it rich with gold and other sources of trade. While they didn't find gold, they discovered land that could be **cultivated** to produce tobacco and other cash crops, such as rice. At first, the colonists in the South weren't interested in cultivating the land. Working the land was too hard and would take a long time. However, the immigrants couldn't survive on the dream of gold.

To ensure the survival of the colony, a man named John Smith stepped in and took control. He made the immigrants work the land. It took longer to make money by raising crops than by discovering gold, but the land provided the immigrants with the opportunity for great wealth. Over time, large farms called plantations were built around the South.

CAPTAIN JOHN SMITH

JOHN ROLFE

POCAHONTAS

John Smith made the rule that those who didn't work in Jamestown settlement, didn't eat. When he left for England, the settlers nearly starved. Later, John Rolfe stepped in and introduced a new kind of tobacco that grew well. Tobacco farming saved the settlement.

SLAVERY COMES TO AMERICA

Before long, farms required additional workers. One remedy was to bring black slaves from Africa. African slaves were forced from their homes, brought to a strange land, and made to work without pay.

In 1619, a Dutch ship carrying 20 slaves landed in America at Jamestown. The use of slaves continued to grow throughout the colonies. By 1790, there were about 300,000 black slaves in Virginia alone.

Indentured servants were another remedy to the labor problem. Indentured servants usually traded three or four years of hard labor for their passage to America. At the end of their term, they were freed. Some indentured servants even earned a piece of land at the end of their term.

SLAVE SHIP

Slaves faced a deadly journey aboard crowded and dirty ships. Once in America, they were bought and sold as property. They lived a life of backbreaking work and no pay.

LIFE IN COLONIAL NEW ENGLAND

The land in the South was rich and ready to farm, but the northern colonies had more trouble. The soil was stony and thin, which made it unsuitable for farming. Many of the immigrants became fishermen and sailors. They settled in areas around the harbors.

BOSTON, CA. 1730

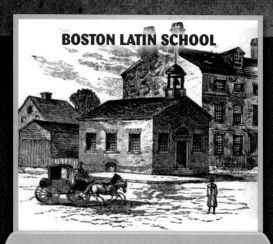

BOSTON LATIN SCHOOL

Boston Latin School promised education to all boys, no matter their social class. It educated many of the early leaders of America, including five signers of the Declaration of Independence.

The towns that grew around these harbors became important centers for business and trade. Education was also important in New England. One law ordered that a school be established in every township of 50 families and that an elementary school be built in the larger towns. Boston Latin School was founded in 1635. It was the first public school in America. In 1636, Harvard was founded in Cambridge, Massachusetts, then called Newtowne. Today, Harvard is still one of the best universities in the country!

THE START OF AMERICAN DEMOCRACY

Democracy was born in America before the Pilgrims even landed. On November 11, 1620, 41 of the men on board the *Mayflower,* docked at Cape Cod harbor, signed the Mayflower Compact. The main idea of this agreement was that citizens would vote on the government and laws, accepting whatever the majority chose. This is one of the first examples of majority rule.

The colonies were supposed to be governed by Britain. However, Britain was busy in wars with France and Spain, so the colonies mostly developed their own laws. Many colonies followed principles and liberties granted in the Magna Carta, a British document from 1215 that assured basic rights to every individual. Most colonies formed their own assemblies that gathered to create laws and give a voice to their people.

SIGNING THE MAYFLOWER COMPACT

The Virginia House of Burgesses was the first elected lawmaking body, or legislature, in the American colonies.

IMMIGRANTS TO THE MIDDLE COLONIES

The middle colonies were known for their religious tolerance. Because different religions were accepted there, the middle colonies had a greater mix of immigrants than did the New England or southern colonies.

The Dutch were among the first immigrants to come to the middle colonies, settling in what's now New York. By 1646, New York had a huge **cultural** mix. The settlers included immigrants from Great Britain, Scotland, Ireland, Germany, Norway, Denmark, France, Poland, and Italy. In 1681, William Penn founded the colony of Pennsylvania. It became a safe place for Quakers and others seeking religious freedom. In 1683, German Quakers as well as families following the Mennonite religion founded Germantown in Pennsylvania. Catholics flocked to Maryland, a colony founded for religious tolerance. Puritans moved to Maryland, too.

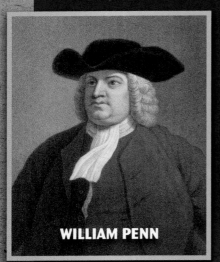

WILLIAM PENN

Because of the many Germans who immigrated to Germantown, there's still a strong Pennsylvania Dutch presence in southeastern and south central Pennsylvania. "Dutch" comes from "Deutsch," which is the German word for "German."

SHAPING A NATION

The 13 colonies grew quickly. By 1700, there were already about 250,000 immigrants living there. This number doubled every 25 years until 1775, when there were more than 2 million people on the East Coast of North America. The level of immigration increased or decreased depending on the quality of life in Europe and, later, in other parts of the world.

Today, immigrants continue to arrive from all over the world to settle in the United States. Just like earlier immigrants, they're in search of a better life free from persecution, fear, and **poverty**. The arrival of people from so many different cultures since the early 17th century has helped make America the democratic society it is today. America is home to many coloful cultures, religions, and traditions thanks to the immigrants who helped shape the nation.

GLOSSARY

cultivate: To raise crops by caring for the land and plants as they grow.

cultural: Having to do with the beliefs and ways of life of a group of people.

democracy: A government by the people.

descendant: A relative of someone from an earlier time.

develop: To grow and change over time.

disease: An illness.

immigrant: One who comes to a country to settle there.

permanent: Meant to last a long time.

persecution: The act of treating someone cruelly or unfairly especially because of race or beliefs.

poverty: The state of being poor.

react: To do something because of something else that happens.

resource: Something that can be used.

tolerance: The act of accepting other ideas, beliefs, or points of view.

INDEX

B
British, 6, 8, 18

C
Columbus, Christopher, 4

D
democracy, 18, 22
Dutch, 6, 14, 20, 21

E
education, 17

G
gold, 10, 12

I
indentured servants, 14

J
Jamestown, 6, 10, 13, 14

M
Mayflower Compact, 18
middle colonies, 20

N
Native Americans, 4, 6, 10, 11
New Amsterdam, 6
New England, 9, 17, 20
New York, 6, 20

P
Penn, William, 20
Pennsylvania, 9, 20, 21
persecution, 4, 9, 22
Pilgrims, 6, 9, 18
Plymouth, 6
Puritans, 9, 20

Q
Quakers, 9, 20

R
religion, 4, 8, 9, 20, 22

Roanoke Island, 6, 11
Rolfe, John, 13

S
slaves, 14, 15
Smith, John, 12, 13
Soto, Hernando de, 5
South, 12, 16
Spanish, 5, 6, 8, 10
St. Augustine, 6

T
tobacco, 12, 13

V
Verrazano, Giovanni da, 4
Virginia, 6, 10, 12, 14
Virginia House of Burgesses, 19

W
wealth, 4, 10, 12
White, John, 11

PRIMARY SOURCE LIST

p. 6
Gezicht op Nieuw Amsterdam (View of New Amsterdam). Created by Johannes Vingboons. Colored print. 1664. Now kept at the National Archives, The Hague, The Netherlands.

p. 10
The Map of All the Coast of Virginia. Created by Theodor de Bry. Engraving. Based on a map by John White. Included in *A Briefe and True Report of the New Found Land of Virginia* by Thomas Harriot, published in London, England, in 1590.

p. 11
Village of Secoton. Created by John White. Watercolor painting. Ca. 1585. Now kept at the British Museum, London, United Kingdom.

p. 16 – 17 (main)
A south east view of the great town of Boston in New England in America. Created by John Carwitham. Hand-colored etching. Created between 1730 and 1760. Now kept at the Library of Congress Prints and Photographs Division, Washington, D.C.

WEBSITES

Due to the changing nature of Internet links, PowerKids Press has developed an online list of websites related to the subject of this book. This site is updated regularly. Please use this link to access the list: www.powerkidslinks.com/soim/colo